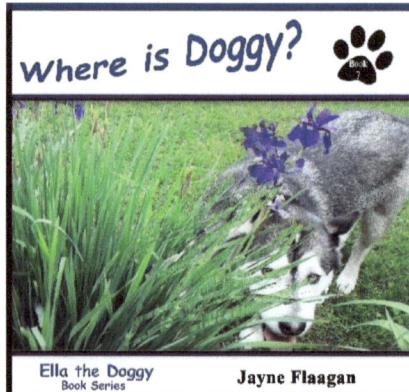

"Where is Doggy "

is dedicated to my friend, **Theresa Wald**,
who inspires me to keep learning and to continue to ask questions.

Jayne Flaagan

Husky Publishing
East Grand Forks, MN 56721
Email: djflaagan@gra.midco.net

Because we appreciate you as a reader, please accept our free, no-obligation gifts to you, which include…

1. Audio sound track of *"Doggy's Busy Day"*

2. Audio sound track of *"Doggy Finds Her Bone"*

3. Coloring pages of Ella to print and color

You will be able to access the audio books and coloring pages immediately when you visit www.ellathedoggy.com

If you enjoy *Where is Doggy?* please leave a review with Amazon.

Sometimes Ella the Doggy is easy to find.

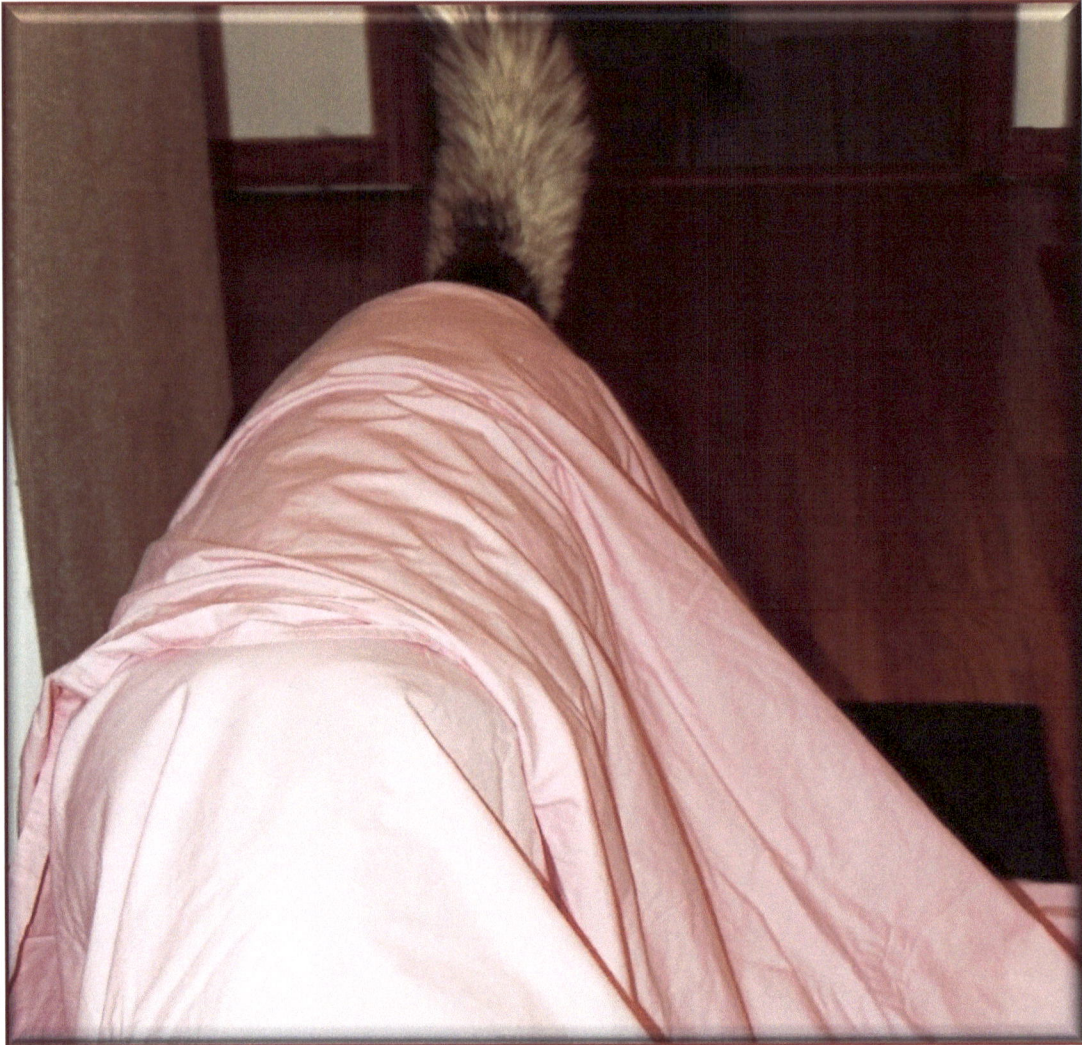

But sometimes she likes to play "hide and seek."

Do you think she knows her tail is
sticking out from under the blanket?

Now her long nose is poking out in front!

Silly Ella!

We knew it was you under the blanket!

When Ella does something naughty,
she hides so she won't get scolded.

Do you ever do that?

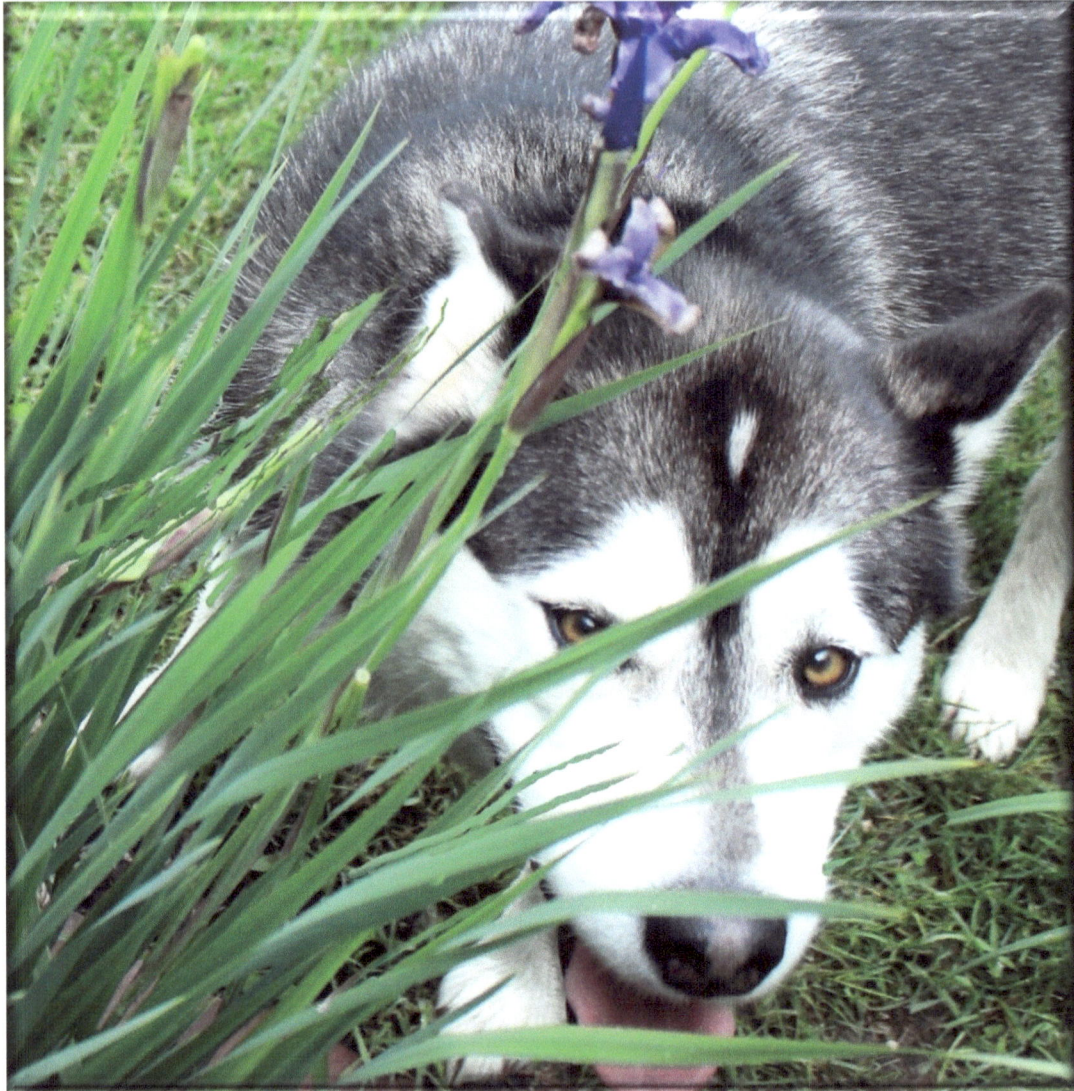

Who is playing *"peek-a-boo"* behind this green plant?

Did you play that game when you were a baby?

Is Ella hard to find in this picture
or is she easy to find?

She's harder to find here, isn't she?

Can you see a red tongue hanging out in this picture?

What else do you see?

Where is that doggy now?

Ella is doing a good job hiding here, isn't she?

Do you see her bushy tail sticking out?

Do you think the man in the red shirt knows
there is a puppy hiding in the bushes behind him?

I wonder if Ella knows we found her hiding spot...

Who is that running through the tall, green grass?

Sometimes Ella gets way ahead of her friends when she goes outside to play.

Look way down this walking path and you will find her!

On this walk Ella found a hollow tree trunk to hide in.

Do you know what the word "*hollow*" means?

You will have to look very closely to find
the puppy behind this big tree trunk!

Is it easier to see her now?

This baby in this stroller will be very surprised when she finds Ella hiding behind her!

Whose head is peeking out around this big garbage can?

Is it the same doggy who is sticking her nose
out around the corner of this building,,,

and coming outside this door?

Now Ella has decided she wants
to come back *inside* the house!

In this picture, Ella is looking out a window.
Can you find her ears, her eyes and her nose?

Where are your ears, eyes, and nose?

Ella the doggy has to say goodbye for now.
We hope you had fun looking for her in the pictures!

Remember to look for Ella in her other books too!

About the Author...

Jayne Flaagan grew up in North Dakota and now lives in Minnesota with her husband and her goofy dog, Ella. She also has three adult children.

Flaagan's experience includes a background of over 30 years in Elementary and Early Childhood education, as well an extensive expertise in writing for many different publications and in several different genres. She thoroughly enjoys writing for young readers.

Books have always been a huge part of the author's life and reading to children is something she feels is critical to every child's learning experience. Flaagan estimates that she has probably read over a million books to children over the years!

The author grew up on a farm with a Husky and has many fond memories of him. Huskies are fun, lovable and have lots of energy! Ella has provided so much joy and entertainment for her own family that Flaagan decided she wanted to share Ella with other families.

Thus, "*Ella the Doggy*" book series was born!

www.ingramcontent.com/pod-product-compliance
Lightning Source LLC
Chambersburg PA
CBHW041239040426
42445CB00004B/86